In Search of Landscape

Also from Sixteen Rivers Press:

In Search
of Landscape

Helen Wickes

SIXTEEN
RIVERS
PRESS

My thanks to the editors of the following publications, in which
several of these poems first appeared: *The Bennington Review,
In the Grove, Pleiades,* and *Runes: A Review of Poetry.*

I would like to express my thanks to the members of Sixteen
Rivers Press; to David St. John and the Whitmaniacs writing
group; to the Bennington Writers; and to my family, friends,
and fellow poets, including Gillian Wegener, Murray Silverstein,
Richard Silberg, Amy Gerstler, Liam Rector, Thomas Sayers
Ellis, April Bernard, Ed Ochester, Ed Smallfield, Eve Pell, and
Babette Jenny.

Published by Sixteen Rivers Press
P.O. Box 640663
San Francisco, CA 94164–0663
www.sixteenrivers.org

Library of Congress Control Number: 2006910001
ISBN(10): 0-9767642-4-5
ISBN(13): 978-0-9767642-4-3

Cover and book design: David Bullen Design
Cover art: Helen Wickes

For Don

Contents

Part One

Scent of Spring

Resumé

I was born in the year of the rat,
under the archer's constellation,

in a house on a hill, the river down below,
and a meadow full of horses, to which,
despite distance and time, I go tethered

my live-long days, fire blessed,
metal weakened, my temperament's curse—
once called the black bile—

fear death by drowning and life
by love, am at the age they call, oh . . .

my volume and density,
not a feather on the expanding galaxy's
latest exhale, this gender's called *other*,

my beloved's the answer, the children
are many, they are stars of a winter night,

and as for religion—I'm a droplet
on the spider's wide-flung web,

in old Norse my name means
where we go hereafter, from the German,
she who lords over the same, but in old Greek,
it's the *torch of flaming oil*,
and rags on a stick, so you can see
your way there and back.

Still Life with a Halter in Its Hand

Sometimes the words appear singly, or in severals,
thrilled to be invited. They leap toward one another
with abandon

but once on the page they stare
blankly into space, where they're from,
or where they'd like to be.

The herd of actual horses stays bunched in the trees.
There are muffled sounds and little puffs
of dust when they stamp their feet.

The one I want comes forward
because of the apple and slips his face
through the halter.

We walk and observe crows on the wire
and the woman in pink curlers walking to the mailbox.
I think about the word *transience*

and imagine tracing the life of writing
in reverse, through its layers—
to rough letters on parchment,

to painted figures dancing across a wall,
drop back to plain red handprints
splayed inside the cave.
I'd like to come forward from there,
stop before the grammar's nailed down,
and find the moment there's a mind

and a hand out of sync. The hand fumbles
to note a sense the image can't evoke,
although whatever it is—*loss, brevity*—

suffuses every figure: *person, horse, cloud, bird*—
the language for abstracting *heart's sorrow*
apprehended, but not set down.

All Must Go for Sale Real Cheap

One guy's work from fifty years back,
these unframed watercolors of a white farmhouse,
here gabled, here by the sea,

next, on a mesa, or in a valley—
at least a hundred, the same house—
assaulted by weather, birds, eucalyptus;

this one with purple wisteria almost lets
some sorrow leak through, but this one
with the slashing branches, Lord, the mood

he was in that day. Pity no one told him
not to use black for shadow
or night; still, he evokes queasy dread

in this cloudbank bearing down. No one
clued him in about translucence,
about paper's desire to shine through paint.

Still, it's all here in this dusty garret
of a shop no one visits but me, and only
when listless, out walking, and I pop in

for a look-see. The beautiful thing
is his signature, in calligraphy, the musical
mid-century name of a mid-century guy.
You can tell he stumbled
into salvation, and left these relics behind—
one man's ticket out of hell. Maybe he

took the class or read the book. He'd drive home
late and couldn't resist picking up the brush.
He'd get it right if he painted one more.

Scent of Spring

One thought does not follow the next.
It rains and the trees rain petals.
Machines are humming throughout the house.

A boy leads a dog with its muzzle tied shut.
Scent of shame on a leash. Rain and wind,
scent of a yellow crocus before it opens.

The man next door, his back to the window,
writes and erases, gets up to eat a cookie,
trailed by the scent of weary pride.

My garage-sale find is a bottle of Tabu,
that scent of remorse with a hint of rage:
A woman preparing for Saturday night,

her black hair and round face and green dress
pretend they love to be together; her mind,
playing without a score, raises the trombone.

The scent of the discarded tunes itself to the imagined;
the ensuing harmonics reveal her life as more
than bearable. Scent of the wildly possible.

Purple

Eyelid and grape hyacinth,
dusk with an iris
in bloom, what's reckless

and raw, bruised on skin,
stain of plum, in the key

of E-minor, for mourning,
at dawn a road
through the desert, what's tasted
beneath the lover's tongue, scent
of violets, plume of distant

smoke, a storm, the unbidden
flush along the throat,
the midnight glow of the psychic's
storefront neon moon,

lilac and cloud shadow,
fragile and persistent

as a ghost if chilled
but glacial if hot,
then purplest prose, jacaranda,
amethyst, whatever's

baroque, ornate, overwrought
and doesn't care what you think,

what's been squandered,
a distillation of scarlet,
crimson ripened, held until
it softens, cries a little
in the hands of blue,

deranged, pushed out
of ethereal, blue
unhinged, off its rocker,
in high gear.

Original Love

I'm Rafferty the poet, full of hope and love,
were the first words of verse I knowingly read,

Blind Rafferty, Irish poet, 1784–1835
or something like that—

Ah, I could read this, and ran for a knife to slide
between the uncut gilt-edged pages,

revealing the lantern-bearing hermit. *My eyes
without sight / my mind without torment.*

Imagine! I thought, no vision, no worry.
The book was scented with leather and time.

I must have abandoned my treasure: Sold, lent out,
or lost, it vanished; the years as well,

the lines occasionally jostled by memory,
going West on my journey / by the light of my heart.

One day at the bookstore—and here, oh no,
Raftery's your true name, I carried you wrong

all these years and now restored—still blind, still rambling—
Tired and weary to the end of the road.

Art History

About beauty they sometimes get it wrong,
don't they, the fine scholars,
bent on instruction? For example, right here

with Rembrandt's *Polish Rider*, they carry on
about *his sorry nag*, meaning *such a loser*,

meaning, because our soldier doesn't ride
a massive, buffed, and snorting charger
(the curators' notion of warhorse, deriving
from pigeon-soiled statues, and the latest

remake of *Henry V*), they tell you
where to read failure—but so what if the horse
is scrawny; look at his rider armed to the teeth

with bows, knives, sword, and ax,
scanning over his shoulder as he hurries, you hope
to safety, though the swallowing murk

of Rembrandt's background refuses comfort
(the horse's legs, states the placard, most likely
completed by the master's apprentice).
You can see the soldier rides

the typical flea-bitten gray Polish Arabian.
This creature may be skinny, but he's fit.
Ignore the critics and trust the horse to get
through winter, survive on snow melt
and whatever gruel the locals will spare.

If you wipe the smirk off your face and put
your feet in the stirrups,
with luck the horse can find the way.

Ode to Stones

I have so many. Serpentine, sandstone,
quartz, and granite—they remind me of
a stone's throw, a thrown stone, an avalanche,

a sand dune and sandstorm at Stovepipe Wells,
the rock that can't stop its rolling,
that pebble in your shoe,

Jack come tumbling with his Jill so quickly;
but a stone can be a shard—insoluble and quiet—
which has a human feel, is a made thing,

that's chipped off sliver by sliver—
as in chip off the old block—his on the shoulder,
hers, under the tongue, like ice;

and out of nowhere at night, as when
a window shatters, or that lonely rock
with his only Sisyphus,

or the down-falling where river rock
runs smooth, washes clean, rocks you
to sleep, 'a-bye-baby,

washes the mote from your eye;
one for you and one for me; and over there,
where there's fresh road cut—

time's diary writ slow, a night-table dream book,
a scribbled-in wish book—
can you read it—from the glacial to the volcanic,

the slow stretch and outcrop
of basin to range, all that's hauled out
from under, hurled down from up;

let's end with the quarried and carted,
what's broken to bits,
so much dirt, so few rubies.

Home of the Lost Poems

I run an orphanage for abandoned poems.
Some remain infants. A few autistic. Many have tossed

their training wheels. On the third floor, those old enough
to vote and drink still want mom to kiss goodnight. Downstairs,
those who secretly reproduce, and oh my! Triplets at dawn.

This poem meant to unlock the rusty gate to the next world.
Which would of course be worth visiting. This to praise
everything before it ends. One that praises before the praiser ends.

The poem to make you fall in love with me. Another to undo spells.
The verse to ward off madness, earthquakes, and children
tossing pebbles. The epic tracking the mind's descent through beta,
theta, and delta waves. A lyric to retrieve said mind.

The creator knew which poem was the fake — one of those
*we lived in the 'burbs, Father ignored us, Mom was weird,
my brother a lout, my sister a gorgeous genius* poems.

This one meant to make the creator seem cool. In the final poem,
imagination leaps — the spider needing little to anchor the silk.

Lives of the Clouds I

John Constable's *Cloud Study*, 1822. The title
says it all, the roiling ones above, the white
and massy below, a few tinged rose, and a cloud
streaked gold rips open into blue.

But no one stops to pay homage, they've gone to see
the alleged Piero (read the small print: *doubtful attribution,
school of*); and it's John the Baptist with his head
still on, then everyone's off to the Annunciation,

and Mary with her stricken schoolgirl look—
Oh, gosh, thank you, sir, but heavens, why me?
I prefer my Mary surly, as in, *Hey, angel, can't you tell
I'm busy.* Over there, a famous flagellation

some enjoy comparing to others—more whipping,
less pathos—but let's stay with these clouds,
where we can't tell, dear viewer, if the view
is out or up or down—no figures, no horizon,

and what's the weather, is it storming, or gusty,
maybe snowing. For an instant, we think it's
an explosion—smoke, dust, and aftermath. And then
we see pure cloud pierced through by daylight,
every permutation illumined from within.

Flutter

Dial the house
of the one who died—
you've done it—
set her phone ringing,
and you're half afraid
someone will pick up,
but it's her voice
you want now,
her machine-trapped
voice saying,
call back later,
leave your name,
I'll get back to you.

The phone keeps ringing,
and the sky's a pink dawn
with black wires strung
in a stave through which
the moon, a whole-note,
falls, decrescendo
behind the rooftops.
You can almost name
the mode it plays in—
Lydian, Aeolian, Ionian?
Something she who died
knows is ridiculous.

Each telephone
sounds identical. No,
every single ring unique;
what stays the same
is this pooled silence

that sounds jump from,
slide back into,
the quiet closing over
the sound.

Sit Still Long Enough, the World Comes to You

I sit on the porch thinking about three types
of fear: *the silver, the pronged, the quivering.*
About eleven of anger, among which: *the pungent,*

the silken. And one joy, like fractured light
through a prism, this fragile intrusion,
one I can't dance to, can't dance with.

It's dark out now, and damn, here you come again,
ghost boy, spirit of my brother forty years ago,
most likely our father eighty years back,

catching my eye, smoky cowlicked wisp of a boy
gliding barefoot, sleepwalker in white pajamas,
fifteen seconds of fog-swirl, then gone. I know you.

A Saint for Each Affliction

White lilies slung over her arm,
as portrayed on a card sold by the nuns,
here's little St. Dymphna,
patroness of nervous

and mental disorders, red curls
snaking past the scarf, her face too stern
for one so young, whatever the harm—
and saints are usually harmed.

But what a nuisance this girl would be
as a daughter. She would flinch
if you barely frowned. Her prayer
asks God to cure—if it be

His will. There's the catch—His whim—
her God keeps an out. But we see
by the notes on your placard that—
ah, my little Irish one—you were steeped

in affliction. Let's hope you shouted
something nasty one moment,
like the rest of us, and in the next,
were snared by beauty. Do you speak

in a divine tongue, do your prayers
flame their way straight to heaven?
Here, carry along a few extra syllables.
You have nothing to lose.

Listen—we're down here lighting match
after match to cheap firecrackers.

Oakland Superior Court

They want me, they want me not.
No, your honor, I'm not impartial.
I will fail to reason with my comrades,
am not unprejudiced, am a creature
of unbridled emotion in a very weak mind,
have a scrawny, walleyed attention span,
a violent fantasy life (you don't want
to know). *Can I just handle simple facts?*
But these facts, sir, or any one alleged fact,
can I paint it orange, fry it in oil,
kneel at its feet, sleep with it tonight,
bathe it in milk, hammer it to smithereens
and bury the teeny pieces under the dogwood,
put a leash around its neck and walk it
downtown? You can see, I'm not, your honor,
the one you want. Take her, take him,
they look to have minds tethered to bodies,
selves with some sense of home in the world;
take them, please, you won't regret it.

Advent Countdown: Open the Windows

Childhood, we say, or loneliness: here they coincide,
there they unbraid. In this window, snow turns to sleet,
blue sparks spray from the train wheels; but when
we open our eyes it's years later,
summer, another city, pigeons in a flurry.

Here's a window in which the father, driving fast,
hits a little dog and makes the kids swear to never,
ever tell a soul, to cross their hearts and hope—
and so in the next window they tell everything
every chance they get, still crossing, still hoping—

Open another window, and oh look, walking four miles
through the snow for a doctor, the mother promises God
that if he spares the sick kid, she'll gladly hand over
pieces of the rest of them—this one's heart, that one's mind.

In one window, the sun puts forth an extra blade
of light. *Daylight*, we venture,
and fret about what will be cut next
from this every so often—
not exactly happiness, but close enough.

Grievance Is My Lot

I care for a dozen little hatreds every day:
They each inhabit a cage with rusty bars;
luckily, they are easy keepers,
thrive on dust, need water
one Sunday a month.

At evening, I turn them loose to annoy
anyone who has acquired a bigger house,
a brilliant book review, who basks in whatever
special glow, and I often let my hatreds rile
the spoiled children. This placates my soul.

I was raised to think a legacy is precious,
each hatred unique.
One has thorns, one has teeth,
another smells so bad I lock it in the pantry,
but my favorite merely scowls;

because they need some looking after,
I sacrifice the remainder of my life
to care for them. Don't pity me—
it wasn't that much of a life to begin with.
And yes, I not only sipped from envy's cup,

I drained it. My pleasure in nurturing
each little hatred is reward aplenty.
Someone offered, for a sum, to rid me
of all my hatreds. No thanks,
I said, they love me so much.

Lives of the Clouds II

As we carried the pail of raspberries,
we thought about fragrance,
and brevity, and about the nature
of clouds. We learned to observe the crows

on the fenceline, the swans on the river.
We considered the birds and what
they meant. Whether it mattered
if next year they meant something else.

White clouds sailed, we said, *in a blue sky,*
as if oared and skippered,
hauling myrrh, pink lilies, or Gregorian chants,
from one horizon's harbor to the next.

When we could learn no more, the loud crows
and stout swans stared back at us.
We blinked and allowed that clouds
were the sky's personality—often cheerful,

clingy, or feverish, though sometimes bored
with their own nothingness. Starved for play,
the sky sculpts a cloud from the damp air
and then tears it apart for fun. And begins again.

Prayer for Autumn with Sparrows in the Margin

Even the birds, Lord, the screeching birds,
how they hover, driven by one desire at a time.

How hunger each moment revs their seed hearts higher.

Give us another day to hide from the birds,
their raw simplicity, which makes us pull the curtain
to escape their eyes.

We'd rather behold than be beholden.

Where, Lord, can we rest when you fill the cup with twilight,
drain it to the dregs, and fill it with dawn,

the garbage truck, the newspaper against the door?

If you insist, we'll open the window,
despite the wish to be no more than a hum

fathoms beyond the driven heart of a bird.

If you insist, we'll look the creature in the eye,
and take his hunger to heart,

but if we do this, spangle us with a desire
or two of our own.

Part Two

Stealing from
the Word-Hoard

Elegy to Saturday Morning in Black and White

(Chuck Jones, 1912–2002)

Long before Keats and that Grecian urn
held any claim, I had my private object
of contemplation: Wile E. Coyote in hottest
pursuit of Mr. *Beep-beep* Road Runner.

No *leaf-fring'd legend*, no *ye soft pipes*
to temper the squeal, the growl, the groan.
World War II barely over, the whole country
hurled itself into capital letters, into the fifties.

My father, ripped awake by a nightmare
about the Nazis, about landing at Anzio,
pale and sweaty and cursing his damned life,
stumbles downstairs for another cold one.

Unlike that urn, the Channel Six cartoons
had no girl to be captured, no heifer's throat
to be cut. Characters set, the ending a lock,
and artistry is all. The master has finished

spinning his ever-changing, ever-constant
background props of cactus, road, cliff,
and drop-off—the dizzying fall into panic
with its sparkling *that's all!* release.

The Road Runner eludes, undaunted, untasted.
But Wile E., full of doomed desire, and yellow-
eyed from humiliation's sting, he's our guy.
Hunger springs eternal. The chase is on.

Cumaean Sibyl

Wasn't she supposed to look different
from the one I keep seeing? Shouldn't she look as if
she'd uncurled her great body
from Michelangelo's too-tight frame, stepped
down, stretched, yawned, and chanted,

or as if kin to a Macbeth witch
in black and white, drooling, marble-eyed,
her claw hands raking the air—anyhow,
granting the round-trip to hell and back—

but no, this one, this sibyl looks like anyone whose life
branches here and there. Keeps branching
and burrowing so deeply into the ordinary
that she becomes strange,
becomes the plump little thing dispensing jokes

for free—mumbling a recipe for lamb chops,
a sure thing for the Del Mar trifecta,
her yimmering, braying, cooing,
to be recorded, sound by unearthly sound,
if you can sit still that long,
then transcribed by hand—these are the rules;

I didn't make them up—then it must be translated
into actual language, and in time,
sent forth. This is where the poem begins.

The Chaperone

My mediocrity accompanies me to the cafe,
coughing gently when I think or speak.

I visit cities, try new occupations,
marry other men, improve my figure,

but no matter—observing my diligence,
it waits, hands in its pockets—

solar storms flare,
briefly disrupting our atmosphere;

governments ascend and collapse
only to reconstitute with great fervor;

while my very own mediocrity sits beside me
during the movie and observes my face,

scientists attempt to define happiness
in order to prove its occurrence;

several hundred species of flower
and bird pass quietly out of existence.

Having acquired the key to my home,
my mediocrity gives a small bow

and opens the door. I go inside, saying,
Okay, make yourself useful, clean the house,

but his lordship my mediocrity says, *Oh please,*
it's such hard work dogging your footsteps.

The Daphne Chronicles

Skin

She exited her tree during the plague year,
bored with memory spinning its concentric
accretions around her damp vegetal core,
a fate she had never fully embraced,
trapped as she was between remembering
and leafing. But because she still had use
of her vestigial mind, human existence
persisted, uncensored in imagination,

a twisted, yellow, sweaty, moaning relic.
The gods said, *What the hell, let's give her
a chance.* Her passage back into personal life
was not unlike the minutes when anesthesia
wears off. Before the morphine drip soothes
the sutured body, murmuring, *There, now.*

Bone

She rarely stays the night, doesn't want
a cab, just evaporates, trailed by a trace
of smoke, crackle of twigs, leaves rattling.
Doesn't have much stuff: a leather dress,
copper nail polish, amber bead in her right ear,
an X-shaped scar on her chest, which she tells
her lovers occurred after surgical excision
of seven supernumerary ribs that grew

until they nearly punctured her breasts.
(Lovers, she learns, are lonely for talk.)
Depending on her mood, she describes the ribs
as having resembled antlers, deep-sea coral,
or valley streams that feed a river delta,
as seen after snowmelt from a great distance.

Teeth

Having mastered the intricacies of love,
the rest of human life bedevils her.
The frantic momentum of legs and feet.
The nonstop sucking and spewing of air.
Sleep—a barren land, tree'd with dreams—
And drama—*Macbeth* has trees! No, only men
pretending to be trees. Seasons—new fingers
won't germinate come spring. And the problem

of eating. Her skin, unlike roots, refuses
to drink in rain. Wriggling in dirt, her toes
transmit nothing. The sun sets no sap flowing.
Photosynthesis inoperative, her skin
will not ever, she wearily reminds herself,
turn green again. She learns to bite and chew.

Blood

She was out for it. Cleansing the language
became her chosen vocation. Advanced degrees
in metaphor vigilance. Seminars, books, symposia,
call-in radio, visiting scholar, you name it,
she was there policing the language, keen to catch
the insult. Whirlwind scourge of the ignorant.
Wherever she found the heedless remark:
flat as a board, sawdust for brains, rail thin,

blown over like matchsticks. Wooden nickel,
rootless, you poor sap, she went to work.
Knock on wood, up a tree. She was a zealot.
Fortunately, she became bored and quit.
Cold turkey. Now she puzzles over kinship—
for instance, between *to leaf* and *to leave.*

Nerve

Growing old is not a pleasure. The wind blows
and she doesn't creak. Her hair appears to be
full of snowflakes. Bit by bit, she loses
the exquisite memory of how she'd become
a tree. Something to do with thwarted desire
and possession. She researches her story
in mythology texts and *voilà!* Recalls
the plea she yelled. Her listener saying,

If you won't quit grousing and embrace
whatever drama we gods dish out, take this.
Before she could bargain—*Bring on the swan,*
assail me with bees, make me a river—
the deed was done. Fingernail to twig,
nerve to sap, but her mind sharp as thorn.

Breath

Having lost her grace, she reluctantly
opens her eyes to history and learns she's
been immortalized for eons. She visits Rome
this summer. Bernini's version not half bad.
She adores the spot where Apollo's hand
indents her skin, the imprint in the marble
so evocative of pleasure, you'd think
It happened like that. So irritating

to hear young women murmur, *Oh, those gods,*
how romantic! She longs for the blackbird's beak,
the bobcat's claw, an ice storm, a rain slick.
And having roots! She begs to be restored.
Too late, sweetheart, that voice from Olympus.
Think your little life is eternally mutable?

Stage Fright

What's my role, am I the star
Is there a plot, any theme, a character
or just someone's lines to memorize
Who's in charge here

Did I write this, am I directing
Can we try this again
The costume's all wrong, get the hairdresser

Send for makeup, and oh God, bring a sandwich
before I eat the script, and who
wrote this, I need revisions

Can I go home now
Wrong lights, wrong darkness, can't see you
Do I hear rustling and excitement
It's me they're here for, isn't it

Do you mean to tell me
I've been doing this every night for years
Remind everyone

I'm allergic to wool and I don't handle cats
I won't kiss him, he's too fat, too old
too young, and no, I won't go on with her

She's too pretty, too smart, too too
I won't say lines that make me sound dull
mean, phony, and stupid,
even if you think I am

All I ever asked was for you to call me starlight,
constellation, galaxy, your sweetest everlasting
Tell me who's out there, what's wanted of us
The blue of dusk to praise it

Plaintive voices of the long gone
the tossed away, swimming back lonely
for a little attention, are they
All right then

Maria Callas: Reliquary

Since they've already thrown her ashes
into the Aegean, let's send her chinchilla coat
to Paris, and why not her ermine jacket,
to Athens, her three still-braided
plaits of hair to Milano, but only Venice
can have the blue corset, and hand over
those fourteen pairs of the finest gloves
to Manhattan, and the black girdle, oh Lisbon
for sure, and as for the rest, give those
high heels and hats and handbags to whomever
wants a piece of Maria under glass. We'll
wait to catch a little night vibrato,
the *come hither, go hence*, in Tosca's glance
before descent—eyes afire, one hand whirling,
just so. But go ahead, bid on anything
you wish. Spread the wealth around.

Glossolalia, the Gift of Gab

From *gloss*, the Greek for "tongue," *see gift*
of tongues (Apostles 2:4, but where's the grammar
in *glossolalia* and does it have a lexicon?),
which is distinguished from *speaking in*

(see Genesis, Chapter 11), which pertains to Babel,
after the tower built in search
of unbroken speech, too high, and whoops,
we're plural again; oh, Noah, your sons and daughters of,

can't understand your babble of. Quick, cut this word
back to *gloss*, which shines, the light's attraction
to the surface of things, and *gloss* the misleading
interpretation—run your fingers down any *glossary*;

peel back quick to *loss*, linger as long as you're able;
peer out through *os*, the smallest aperture of all,
and build yourself back up to *osteo*, rib from,
bone to, marrow of, not the marrying, avoid *ossify*

by swerving sideways to cousin words, like *gossip*—
which comes from *godmother*, the infant's sponsor
in the rite of baptism. Digress again, you're in *gospel*,
its origin being "the stranger's tongue."

Oh, there's too much lability. We're back at *lalia*,
from Greek, for tongue, see *Babel* above, later meaning,
"the foreigner's speech," as in, *You're not*
from around here, lady, are you? But wasn't that

the good book's promise—aim our prayers upupup
and our fractured speech flies straight to heaven?
It ain't so, as the old song goes, and since he breaks
your heart in two, over and over, speak from them all.

Chronicle of Cain

Turning this way and that in the mirror,
I keep wondering how to be as golden
as my brother Abel. I comb my hair
a little differently. Fig and grape, wheat

and barley, I hold my breath and harvest
my fruit and gather my grain.
Some are kissed, others not, I can tell,
walking into any room, how it will be.

And so I watch the way Abel,
the favored son, picks the plumpest, cutest lamb,
and I learn how he brings death to it,
swiftly to beauty in its prime.

Father's hand lazily drops down from the clouds,
picking, picking . . . whatever he wants
from my brother's choicest cuts, but not my fruit,
or my grain into which I poured my sweat.

The road home curls behind me
like altar smoke. Mothers and fathers lean down
to their children and whisper my story.

What I most regret is stomping all the figs
I'd grown. How sweet they would have tasted.

Translating Emily Dickinson

At the twentieth-century's turn—
a retired civil servant
passed the years in his Chinese village,

hunched over dictionary and primer,
staring hard into *certain Slant of light*,
then out the window, but still he wrestled with—

peculiar angle of steep-pitched knife-thin winter rays,
not sure if he even came close,
then *Heft of Cathedral Tunes*—took days

to render *Temple dinner gong*, the sound,
weighty as an ox—into something pleasing,
and then burrowed into *We can find no scar,*

but internal difference, where—
fast as he wrote, he crumpled his own—
Sleeping carp, no moon, frozen lake—

not right, although—*First concubine's
third daughter's lost jade, wrong lover,
and lynx on the prowl* was worse—

so he stopped to holler at his cat, and wondered about
But internal difference, Where some—
no, *the*—*Meanings are, None may teach it,*

and scrawled—*my mother gone, my father gone,
no one else to remember them*; he wiped his pen,
put away the ink, saw his way, and thought:

behind my fourth rib—this image of heat
and smoke—and wrote—*in the ice-sharp night*—
two figures light their pipes.

**Upon Completing His Painting Entitled _Madame X_,
John Singer Sargent Thinks about Talking with His Favorite
Sister, Emily, a Fellow Painter, in His Paris Studio, 1883**

No other jewels, I told her, _we will set off that pallor_,
which as you know, she heightens with a good dusting
of lavender powder. The all of you, I didn't tell her,
trussed up by ornament. But Emily, I've got it, haven't I?
The strap of her dress lists off her right shoulder—
twist of pearl, gold foil—a trifling jeweled thing

nibbling the skin of her plump, undamaged arm.
Not reckless what I've done? She's eccentric in style,
an arriviste, parvenue. With no real daring, not like Mother—
oooh, children, off we go, to Florence—but do you
like the dress, black, verging on aubergine? Her beauty,
what can I say—I stare. And flinch. Is of a dusky plum,

won't dry into a prune's sweet leather, but will spoil
at once, without a trace. Nothing worked. I tried her
on chaise, on sofa, twisting her arms. Here, I have her
leaning on the table, her arm torqued; its weight spirals down.
I tried the pose myself. It felt spectacularly tentative.
But some days—damn them, these ladies, and damn this one's

right ear, this flaw, I painted a too-pink little object coiled
against the head, but some of Mother in the bosom's plunge
to seemingly nowhere. Lord, I pity a beautiful woman's son.
Happiness to these people? They find it cheap, requiring
a surrender that's been bred out of them. I long for sunshine,
a tramp along the sea with you. Remember that gypsy woman—

poor and drunk and slovenly and glorious—I painted last year
in Venice? Wonder if she's alive. She was so full of her life that it
poured off her. You could scoop the vitality with your brush, paint

with menace and grace. But Madame X—her beauty is milky,
marbled—no, chalky—like the Dolomites. She exudes chilled air,
as breathed off of new snow. Her sorrow lives in this gray pool smudged

beneath her eyes to which viewers will return for repeated sips.
I doubt that she is loved. Someday, enough of the gorgeousness
I'm hired to serve, much as the governess or their butler. I do
their dogs, their brilliant children, make them all goddessy.
When are you coming? I want you to see the glow—of gentian
past bloom—I've laid along her throat. Will you like it?

Grendel's Brother

So. They're gone now,
my dam and my only brother. Taken
from me. Into the unliving, I guess.

We are frightened by night, so no wonder
we frequent the far-off castle, lit
from within. (Lit, I suspect,
by sunshine, which humans have taken hostage,

        and subdued there.) Pulled as we are
to mead-halls, Mother and Brother for the sport and food,
but me for the goings-on, the torchlit sight
of gold on a woman's neck, for the glimpse
of creatures at their ease, pouring themselves
into song and speech. Even their grief
has a word-weaver. Their dogs

sniff me out and howl, their horses whinny,
humans never see me: *softened stone,*
we're made of, *the hardened fog as well.*
I stare and listen. And steal

        from their word-hoard.
I memorize what are called things, how the words
shade and qualify. Suggest and deny. And so

though I'm not written into the story, can't you
feel me, this margin-prowler, this haunter
of mid-line pauses, the throat-catch
as you turn the page?

2

Every lullaby, sea-chant,
serenade, wedding ode, war salvo, burial dirge.
Bard's creation song too. I know
by heart. How they sing

      about us: Hell-reaver, Hell-dam,
harrowers of earth, they call us,
but what about me—monster who whimpers,
moor-coward, sissy of the kesh, lurker,
loser, misbegotten kin of Cain
dreaming his way. Quickened earth,
we are. But I'm last

        of my kind, don't fancy
the female human. Peeling off her pelt
to bathe and sleep. Not like my mam.
Sending me out to avenge
my brother. How can I? With what?
Slinking to the moors I mourn.
Then her as well, her lease-hold snapped,

3

left me missing their voices:
Swipe us a few brook-salmon,
go break the fragrant branches
for our beds, mind your brother, catch me
a squirrel, she orders,

      I obey. Cowering. Cheerful.
Proud of the treasure-trove of speech
I give them—with which she growls
for more purple berries
plucked from brambled thickets.

We're made from calcinated water: These words I gave them,
plus another nine hundred seventy-six.
Without me, they grunted
and snarled, in just eighty-three sounds,
to be exact. *You're not like us,*

        Grendel said, *you can't stalk, can't*
hunt, can't seize. You inspire
no fear. You have small feet.

Which I do, but always meant to tell him,
We are the sublimated bronze.
Go bring fresh eggs

        from the rushes
and not to break a one, he called—he was her bairn,
her cub raiding the castle,
rousing fate. Who'll roust me now
from the mere, who will poke my ribs
to beg a ballad? Grabbing sweet kernels
of walnuts I shelled as they gobbled

my words. Dragon-bounty
of luminous speech. *Th* a real trial,
pl was too. They puffed and blew, but a little language
made them greedy for more.

    4

        The tempered stone we are,
or the coagulated smoke.
That last one sounds better, don't you think?

Martha Jane Canary, Known as Calamity Jane, on Her Deathbed, Calloway Hotel, near Deadwood, South Dakota, 1903

Martha Jane, I, Canary—called Calamity,
because where Hell rises—there I,

a whirlwind rouser be. Misfortune trailed me
the way a porcupine tail swings through dirt.

My poor old mind like a summer's lightning,

which drops a steer to the ground, moves on,
and sets a tree to fire, moves on.

Yes, I succumbed to vices, but better those
than the diseases I nursed you people through:

smallpox, diphtheria, cholera. And the eyes
of your children asking of me, *Lady, what's next.*

It's been said that long ago I was pretty.

I too have seen my own face in passing.
Hello, Calamity—you old fog across the glass.

I went to Texas to run cattle, to Colorado
for haying, Oregon for horses. Left my only
girl child to those nuns for good schooling.

Returned to see my Bill Hickok's grave.
I'll be with him in eternity. When that day comes,

bury me in white, *head to foot in my glory robes.*
Won't I be a sight for your bitter eyes?

But one last time, load a pistol, hold up a card,
let me shoot it from your fingers. *Remember me.*

I was the fancy dancer who could heat your toes

and shiver your mirrors. I owned a brown horse
name of Satan, and then my freckle-dog, Blue,
and once I had a mother.

Part Three

What the Eye Can See

No Epiphany on Mt. Diablo

Just hatched and fully formed,
a baby rattlesnake,

his little mouth a long O;
his body whips and ribbons

as if he needs to shed
something unbearably itchy.

There must be hundreds
more of him; no such thing

as an only-child snake. His eyes,
brilliant as just-found stars

whose luster we happen upon
light years from their conception.

Halfway down the peak,
two coyotes saunter through a herd

of Herefords, as if auditioning
for herd-dog jobs.

The snake quits seething
and stares. What exactly does he see?

I think about crushing him but don't,
from fear, not kindness.

The rattle of his tail accompanies me
through the landscape of pasture

and vineyard, suburb and city,
flickers through the keys in my hand.

Feather

A solitary rower
sets out in a
slow hurry down

a long lake,
dusk a quick mood,
night happens

fast, hope he knows
what he's doing.
We could look for

his face
through binoculars,
his coppery sunset

backlit face,
which would be
a sort of trespass,

wouldn't it.
Often I think
about boats

with nobody in them,
or a boat plus person,
no oars, adrift

in a terrible quiet,
frogs mouthing
blue-back flies,

but mostly I see
one oar floating,
slung and slapped

by the current,
but how it floats,
love, it floats.

Either Way, the Wind Came Up

The breeze ratchets up an octave.
I wait it out on a rock.

The sound exhausting and demanding as a long illness
only patience or cunning will cure.

Time for once doesn't hurry up or hold still
or turn back. With its branches stripped by drought,
the creosote tree looks dead but isn't.

Someone's unknotted this wind from a handkerchief corner.
I'll give thee a wind.   Th'art kind.   And I another.
I myself have all the other.
Get out of here, weird ladies, I know your tune.

The wind quits in a huff. The small, nameable sounds return:
breath, bird wing, the click of a few grains of sand.

The quiet soothes, like a hand on the forehead.
I almost have something to say

about moments springing open.
The earth hath bubbles, as the water has,
And these are of them.

By a sleight of hand, an offstage smirk, dread creeps in
and rubs shoulders with tranquillity. Fraternal twins,

only one of them keeps his shades on and rips his name tag off
at the door. Sneaks through every time.

The dread not of silence here, but silence there. Past the Salton Sea?
No, farther. How much? Past the moment one leaves or one is left.

Would prefer nerves of steel, heart of gold.
Will compensate with wonder about things: *microfleece, malarkey,*
flapdoodle, homesick. Miles from the road,
I sit on a rock and watch a green lizard.

Borrego Journal, Thursday

I'm fond of dodder, that plantlike parasite that drapes a cloud
of orange webby tendrils and small white flowers
over its host, extracting what it needs

to live. A voice broke into my delight, saying, *Break the one
into many, let pillars of dust arise, let the dry sponge drink*,
but I didn't listen. I walked around

a creosote plant. To survive for hundreds of years,
to outlive the drought, its roots descend forty feet. Willingly,
it drops its glossy leaves to keep living.

Existence or vanity—how lucky to have a choice. Everyone
comes to Kendall's for breakfast. The coffee's okay,
the newspaper has news of tanager sightings

and C.P.R. classes. Good thing. Last night a man
at the next table fell over. Someone said *choke*, someone said
stroke, someone said *heart*. He lived, but for seven minutes,

the room was silent except the clock tick-ticking.
It could have been you or me, turning blue,
one slippered foot sliding over the threshold.

Borrego Journal, Saturday

On the east side of the valley,
there's a piano player who growls,
Now for some romance, as he jabs at the keys

as if to get back at Ellington for writing
what he, what we, can't ever create, but still
we clap our hands because the man is lonely

and sour, and bloody well lucky to get four nights
to tinkle the keys at the El Zorro Bar
just south of Borrego Springs. Outside and flying

over the Santa Rosa mountains en route
to the Salton Sea, the Angel of the Stolen Bells
repeats her demand for fresh-cut barley, as much

as six burros can haul to Santa Ysabel,
and maybe at last she'll say where she's hidden
the bells. They were stolen in 1926.

People say they hear them ring every midwinter,
iron tongues loosened by cold. Bright
and inscrutable as starlight.

So ring, you stolen bells;
piano man, keep plonking away; and Milky Way,
lift us up with your cold and burning light.

In Search of Landscape: A Poem in Twenty-One Parts

Scape

Lord, if you rid me of these blues,
I promise you, *no more moons* in the poem,
neither the sliver nor the wedge. So please
rescind these walking blues,
and I'll hand you unlunared radiance,
neither the fattening moon nor the slendering.
I'll leave unwritten the chalky, milky,
and marbled, won't natter on about bathing
in its pearly, won't pour it over my shoulder,
won't search there for the muse, for you,
for whatever isn't. I'll forget old moon,
hanging in the closet, unveiled,
star sprinkled, and cold.

Landscape

My compass needle atwitter, the two norths
converge under glass in my hand;
the vanishing point turns inward. The body
at high altitude wheezes and gasps for air;
the air plays hard to get. Each step forward
breaks the visual frame, which my eye recomposes.
I watch my patient feet hauling my mind,
which can't be quiet, can it?
See the mind describe the feet—two shuffling boats,
no? Little porters? But what if we're lost,
who will miss us? Ah, there's the car.
One more day accomplished.
One less day to live.

Seascape

It's comforting to know that the seascape
is out there, handling the continent,
saying, *How about I rearrange
your figure?* But here there are lakes,
and lakes have moods, not tides.
Everything *gets* to a lake.
A lake's not river directional,
spring discrete, or ocean endless.
The lakescape's at the mercy
of boats, fish, light, in thrall
to the clouds, the air, complete in itself,
but begs the moose to wade
right on in and calm its nerves.

Landscape

Now, it's cattle-moving time
of year, and here they come,
the rusty sluggish river of them
down-mountain for winter.
Horses and three dogs
are about their business,
the guys on their cell phones.
The cows play the game,
their calves recalcitrant
and bawling, hysterical, slip-
sliding on the asphalt. Simmer down,
sweet things, nothing bad
will happen to you
this week.

Mindscape

Shall we raise the door latch and descend
to the crowded dining room for dinner?
I'd rather not, but okay, I'll try. We can
be realistic or figurative. Think
of small talk as makeup,
learned in the safety of home,
wiped off gently before bed.
It won't kill us; the effort will give us
a pearly afterglow. Listen to the sound
of voices rising from the parlor,
how they sound forest-thick, branching,
and brambled underfoot this evening, twining
and thorning and flowering.

To Landscape

All verb now — to plant, contour,
hedge, sculpt, select stones
for the wall, divert streams,
to wind a path to a nook with a bench
for seeing, and call the place
Arcadia, meaning, no need
for maps, water, or a quirky compass.
Imagine first adorning the land,
not for eats, not for shelter,
but for sheer pleasure. Imagine Eden
with all the naming accomplished,
the temptation on hold, and Hell
not yet invented to frighten us.
Fast-forward and now you're stuck
with the upkeep, fertilizing, weeding,
and thumbing through catalogues,
with pests galore. What the heart sometimes wants
is *Wuthering Heights* without
the difficult people, just gorse and wind,
memory, omen, and promise.

Inscape

That's what the words chisel toward,
flinging debris as they go. As after
the August fires, what's left
of the forest is the upright bones
and white ash; we stand knee-deep,
imagining backward and forward.
The Sawtooth Mountain ridge, unburned
for now, resembles a blade,
hand-beveled. I once knew a blade
like this—obsidian married to elk horn
by a thin sinew—the knife's person
showed it to me once at dinner,
as he held forth on the deer-skinning craft
while stroking his hand-sewn shirt,
as fine as a second skin;
his was the mindscape worn outside
for show. Look now, the setting sun
slides its thumb over the ridge, and
draws blood as it tests for sharpness.

Allegorical Landscape

In the world of skinny lodgepoles,
only the plump trees become infested
by beetles and then slowly die.
What remains is a forest of young, tall,
thin, healthy, perfect trees rasping
against each other, clawing for sunlight.
Many will die for want of light,
but of those trees that survive,
regrettably, some will fatten.

Cityscape

How to paint it, how to sculpt it—
your city–how to tell about it
when you're not there. Especially after watching
the Basque sheepherder, his one dog,
his blue roan horse, his wagon with a curl
of blue smoke, his high-desert spot where he lives
all summer, until the flatbed arrives
to haul his whole outfit south.
Tell me about your city, they asked,
so I tried this: *The tongue of morning
was tasting the fog*—no, and tried:
*The lips of dawn kissed the concrete teeth
that scrape the sky's skin.* The people
scratched their heads. I failed them.
Then I won them, saying: *A big-enough city
creates its own weather*—
eddies of clammy heat, pockets
of storm, fierce wind puddles.
A big-enough city speaks a language
that is lean and sturdy, muscular
with rush and roar, is oceanic
and tidal—but alas, if not moon driven
(see "Seascape"), what heart (of ours)
do we hear motoring it along?
At dawn, my city of bridges arches its back.

More Landscape

The word crossed the water from Dutch
to English in 1598 for *rendering in paint the view
from a single vantage*, usually scenery
minus war, bad meals, quarreling relatives.
Did that emigrant word (not serf, not slave,
possessing no green card) shimmy the mast, shout
at the sight of land? Did it care that people
began to call vistas *landscapes*, that it spawned
two genres — seeing and art — each one schooled
and celebrated? Composition is everything.
The lightning strike is an upended tree; this poem
stole its shape from August, from a swath
of forest burning across Montana. So many flames.
Looks like God is trying to herd them,
to create a stampede, that bad movie staple
in which art meets wild and uncoils its lariat.

Scapegoat

It's easy to become one. You've got
what it takes; it's an art form.
See "Escape," which hasn't happened
yet. Remember the annual goat,
the biblical one chased
from the villagescape into wilderness —
long before it became landscape (let alone,
landscaped) — anyhow, the chosen goat bears away
everything, even bad music, or the too-quiet mood
at inedible meals, or the sprung tears
of sad children. Since the heart hungers too,
face the mirror and dab on a few spots
of your best talk; come down to dinner
with me and say anything. I promise you
that things will work out.
If they don't — little hooves
will scrabble the shale, little bells
sliver the night. They'll run us both
out of town, but we'll be together.

Scape

Come on in, child, before the sun
burns the face off your head;
there are bits of fleece on the barbed wire,
and as it should be, the whole land
unfurls to sedge and swale, oh sugaree,
it's a damp night in a bang-up time of it,
the ungrieved creeps forward, open-eyed
and marveling at so much space.
She said there'd be days like this,
and there'd be hard things, like waiting,
and the sadness that scrapes the skin.
Scape yells out for a prefix.
Any needle can be stroked head to heel
with a piece of silk and magnetized
when your compass gets lost. Avoiding wisdom
becomes a profession, ill paid, rarely photographed,
but tenured, indentured, and amply fed.

Cape

I was meant to be Zorro
and swirl around in a black cape,
which was the entire southern night.
I was meant to have a black horse,
lace at my throat, and be great
with a sword. The sword was a river
of moonlight, and I was meant to be
the only one permitted to sail it.
Underlings would warn me of enemies.
I'd drink sherry from a silver vase
and break off hunks of peasant bread
every week or so. You would be waiting
at the window, one of those
leaded-glass casement affairs, draped
with red roses, and I would carry you off,
but alas, by the time I met you,
the cape was moth-eaten, the horse
is blood bay, I have a bad back,
and my language is the closest thing
I'll get to a sword in this life.

Ape

They scare us, those lumbering things,
grunting and swaying. The older we get,
the more we resemble them, thick browed,
scowling, scratching, groaning,
wanting soft food, painfully aware of status
and insects, looking around in wonder
at the peevish human world.

P

Plosives, the sounds are called.
Nope, says the dad, *no Popsicle*.
Yep, says the mom, *pink's what
you're putting on, like it or no.*
Pretty as Parmigiano sprinkled on top,
polite as parsley sitting on the side.
Map, says fourth-grade Miss Turner,
slapping the air with the word as if
it were wet wash on the line. *Landscape*,
snaps the prim little painter, shivering
from the barbarity of it all, preferring
her pavement and glass. And back to basics,
here comes baby babbling his little plosives,
his iridescent, pre-word bubbles of delight.

Land

Maybe Frost was wrong about us belonging
to the land before it was ours. Romantic
notion. So much longing in that word:
Belong to me. And me to you. Landed gentry,
that's what I'd like, my place in the sun,
a cornerstone to mark the boundary, a faded deed
in loopy script three hundred years old,
an ancient, groaning tree to someday relinquish.
Wait, shut me up, I must be channeling an ancestor—
back to your potato patch, Uncle Peregrine.

Summer Landscape

Meadow	Tree	Light	Road	Clouds	Afternoon
River	Ferns	Often	Forest	Path	Shadow
Pebbles	Later	Bees	Sun	Horizon	Drowsy
Grass	Leaf	Flower	Heat	Breeze	Butterfly
Cool	Bird	Valley	Lake	Scent	Green
Thirst	Throat	Dust	Again	Sky	Meadow

Stone Lichen

Feather Clearing

Escape

That's what the fool language is always trying
to do behind my back. It's what happens
to the view if I don't hurry up and stop now,
and jot it down fast. I know full well
how every morning the fogbank withholds
a hidden world just dying to reveal itself,
and right before it does—poof—evaporation.
Whatever secret was there, it wasn't meant
for me. When I ask for sleep to linger awhile,
it flees out the window and over fields,
leaving a trail of telltale streaks. Nothing left
but to greet the dawn and try again.

Another Landscape

If lightning's the kiss and the wind
is pure devotion, then this forest
is ripe for the taking. The fire takes
what it wants for days, for weeks,
making a ruthless revision. The fire jumpers
are angels in reverse, their small planes
borne through heat toward the flames
as if to rescue the damned. You'd almost
call it beautiful. The firefighters
stoke the back blaze, are birds in a gyre
not of their making. Fifteen wild turkeys
escaping the conflagration look both ways
and cross the road, the brains not yet
bred out of them.

Scapegrace

There's scoundrel air and smoke for miles.
They say you can't do art about landscape
because it's done for, the land being
dead, the gaze gone passive, the eye
is jaded, the looking's uncool, the view's
elite, and oh, feather me out
of this rascal time, old star, dry flower.
The whole globe's in a spiral vapor,
the maker stays in his watching place.
Lapidary, the light he sends us.

Grace

Praised be the leafless stalk,
the feather shaft, the declination
between true and arctic north.
The gray horse crossed the hill;
with his pewter gleam, the flick
of his tail, he passed from view,
from his life. You could hear
hoofbeats, then less, then nothing.
We arrive at this meadow of air,
little breezes flow out. Capillary.
The streams of them moving
through the day. Graze upon it.
All that's ripe boils down
to a plum-sweet ghost of itself.

The Spirit's a Silver Needle

It's pulling the tensile thread of us;
we admire the stitches, loops, and knots,
crosshatched and doubled back, the places
of error and grace. Daily life intrudes—
the violet sprawl of curbside lantana
and one red tulip so out of place
it's perfect. The woman with the three-legged dog
cuts across the frame, both of them smiling.

My sharp-pointed mental needle pauses.
The thread breaks. *Make a knot*, I think,
and *cut clean*. Awash in the ongoing,
such a thin stalk of nerves the unwieldy brain
sways on. Reedy and porous mind, you sun-stealer,
droplet-bearer, you bringer of tidings
I barely register.

But oops, the needle sometimes pierces,
blood-jumping the mind awake, this time
to *Zhivago's* final scene. We're back,
you and I, in Louisville, maybe '68, anyhow,
that girl walks away from Alec Guinness;
he's finished telling her all he knows
about her, which is really nothing,
then there's the crummy music and his sadness,
watching her sewn back into the crowd,
and you, gone now too, saying, back then,
That's a real ending.

Narrativity

The setting forth
The crumpled map
The grumble followed by sulk
The nerves, the nerves

The heat, the dust, the light
Sudden exhilaration
The unnameable lily

The unwrapping of tiny candies
The weirdness of having a body
The inexplicable sorrow
The pettiness of taxonomy

Ecstasy of paper and pen
Nothing at the core

The peevish phrase erased
The yeah, then maybe
The solace of pale green

Bath accompanied by snack
The sniffing of the wine
The button, the lace, the snap
The night inside the night

Racket of bluebirds
The no more days
The disheveled bed
Trepidation of skin
The salt and slide of it

In the hereafter, or maybe not
Are we waiting, are we rushing
The map uncrumpled

These purple figs
The horizon, its onrush
The heat, the dust, the light

An Indigo Bunting in Flight

Is not azure, is not turquoise,
more like a hint of the Caribbean, thirty miles east
of Miami, ten in the morning, January 1954,

everyone loved in that moment still breathing,
still complaining about the weather and the cost of living.

The bird, off course from his migratory trail,
flickered past, a shred of torn sky, an elusive memory pool
that I'd gladly now place hands together

and dive straight into. The bird is quick,
and violet around the beak and eyes. He warbles, flits,

and repeats himself in the updraft. The mind wants
a signature hue, the echoing fragrance to keep it going:

bird, moss, lapis, the cotton dress she wore,
only to market. *The bird*, she said, *is not what you think
you see*. The bird is black, its feathers deflecting

and concentrating the scatter-shot sunlight down
into this blue, this deception
I willingly enter.

January Meditation

Late light and what the eye can see,
snow in heaps collapsing off the roofs,
one bird in the red berry bush.
I try to call, but, you know, the phone.

The icicles are something, aren't they,
drippy things marking a tapered, failed
descent one drop at a time, small thoughts
the mind can hold. Toothy and fragile.

Beneath the icicles the tracks of a squirrel
turn blue. I am peering across the shadows,
it seems through slats of grace.
Abide with me here—no, anywhere you choose.

Cheerful Defense of the Realm

Once I used to be and desperately wanted,
but in the beginning I wondered,
though once upon a time I secretly knew.
At first I declared; then I believed.
After a while I noticed, but not enough.
In the end I still wanted. In the middle
I was lost, very lost. In the meantime
I complained. As a general rule I felt.

When it was over, I gently explained
how I had guessed according to the stars.
Apropos of nothing I apologize.
With hindsight I throw up my hands in praise.
Under the circumstances, I'll take another.
Given a second chance, I'd choose the blue.

"Still Life with a Halter in Its Hand" was inspired both by Larry Levis's "Elegy with a Bridle in Its Hand" and by the Polish poet Zbigniew Herbert's essay "Still Life with a Bridle," which in turn comes from a painting by the Dutch painter Torrentius (1589–1644).

"Original Love" was inspired by Anthony Raftery (1784–1835), the blind Irish poet, born in County Mayo, who lived as a wandering bard, fiddle player, and singer, and who appears in W. B. Yeats's poem "The Tower."

"Cumaean Sibyl": The original sibyl was an ancient Greek soothsayer whose shrine was in southern Italy, and whose prophesies were inscribed on leaves. She was said to have guided Aeneas on his journey through Hades.

When John Singer Sargent (1856–1925) created the portrait of Madame X, he painted one dress strap sliding down the subject's shoulder, which prompted such an outcry that he repainted the strap.

"Grendel's Brother" was inspired by Seamus Heaney's 2001 translation of *Beowulf.* I couldn't help but imagine that the monster, Grendel, had a brother.

Calamity Jane (Martha Jane Canary, 1852?–1903) was a historical figure about whom we have few specific facts. It is believed that she practiced nursing after the Civil War and was a teller of tales.

"Glossolalia" is the product of a late-night insomniac romp through the dictionary.

Both the form and feeling of "Summer Landscape" were inspired by Robert Duncan's "Passages 13" from *Bending the Bow.*

DONALD STANG

HELEN WICKES lives in Oakland, California, where for
many years she worked as a psychotherapist. She has a
Ph.D. in psychology and an M.F.A. from the Bennington
Writing Seminars, where she was the recipient of the
Jane Kenyon scholarship. Her poems have appeared in
ZYZZYVA, Runes, Santa Clara Review, 5 a.m, Pleiades,
and other journals. *In Search of Landscape* is her first
book of poetry.

SIXTEEN RIVERS PRESS is a shared-work, nonprofit poetry collective
dedicated to providing an alternate publishing avenue for San Francisco
Bay Area poets. Founded in 1999 by seven writers, the press is named
for the sixteen rivers that flow into the San Francisco Bay.

SAN JOAQUIN · FRESNO · CHOWCHILLA · MERCED · TUOLOMNE ·
STANISLAUS · CALAVERAS · BEAR · MOKELUMNE · COSUMNES ·
AMERICAN · YUBA · FEATHER · SACRAMENTO · NAPA · PETALUMA